T0208923

GIGI CANZONI

WESTBOW
PRESS®
A DIVISION OF THOMAS NELSON
& ZONDERVAN

WestBow Press books may be ordered through booksellers or by contacting:

WestBow Press
A Division of Thomas Nelson & Zondervan
1663 Liberty Drive
Bloomington, IN 47403
www.westbowpress.com
1 (866) 928-1240

ISBN: 978-1-9736-9601-8 (sc)
ISBN: 978-1-9736-9600-1 (hc)
ISBN: 978-1-9736-9602-5 (e)

Library of Congress Control Number: 2020912296

Print information available on the last page.

WestBow Press rev. date: 8/13/2020

Keep readin'

Keep singin'

Keep dreamin'

May the rhythm in your heart always keep beatin'

JoAnn, Dana, Rachel, and Lynn –
Thank you for all the love and support
through this amazing journey.

About The Author/Songwriter

Gigi was born in Melrose Park, Illinois, raised in Chicago, and attended high school, beauty school, and college. Her major studies and achievements follow her with the induction of the National Music Honor Society, National Art Honor Society, President's High Honor Role List with a 4.0 GPA in Business Management, and an Illinois License of Cosmetology. Gigi has an ambitious drive, and known to be a "dreamer." Her love for art and music run deep in her veins. Whether on paper, on stage, behind the chair, or in her ear, she always finds a way to express her passion. Gigi loves people and continues to stride and leverage her hard work, skill, talent, and experiences, through positivity – not only in her own day to day life, but also with the people around her. Music and art is a natural way for Gigi to connect with people on an intimate level, with the goal of touching people's hearts in a way it has touched her own.

Contents

Introduction

Hi, I'm Gigi. Now, you might be thinkin' - Why am I readin' some random girl's journal?

Well, let me fill you in on what you're about to dive into.

Since I was a little girl all I ever wanted to do was make people feel good. I had it set in my head that I was going to be a hairdresser and make everyone feel beautiful. Now, growing up in an Italian-American family in Chicago, being a hairdresser was I guess you could say, "The Norm." Surrounded by hairdressers growing up, that was my way into pursuing something that I love. I had other talents and passions too, but didn't know how to use them towards my goal, into a career. My ability to sketch freehand into art turned into a hobby. Sure, I could have gone to the Art Institute if I wanted to, but I couldn't connect it with how I wanted to connect with people, so I utilized my artistic ability into the beauty industry. Then there was my passion and love for music. I never really had the support or guidance to turn that into a career, it's just always been a part of me naturally. I loved being on stage. I was always in school plays, and travelled with my concert choir putting on different productions. My favorite show was singing at the Museum of Science and Industry during Christmas time. I attended Catholic school growing up, and loved singing in the church choir in my neighborhood. Music was with me everywhere I went. I couldn't be in a car without singin' to the radio, or sittin' in my room with my boombox turned up, or headphones in my ears. When I was a kid, I would get so excited for Saturday nights. Made sure I had my blank cassette ready and pressed record when the mixes came on the radio. I connected everything in my life to a song. Sometimes I would take a song on the radio and alter the lyrics in my head to fit a situation happening in my own life thinkin', what could this sound like if it came from me? That's just how my brain works. I was a songwriter and didn't know it. My connection to music brought me comfort and could never be changed or taken away, even though everything else around me was. There was no medicine that could relieve me of my anxiety; the only remedy was music.

You're probably wonderin', why am I publishing a book and not singin' on a stage somewhere or recording? Like a recording artist, this is my way of sharing my music with people. My journal is my album – but unlike a music album, mine is filled with the heart of my songs. Some of my beats are long, some are short. Like a journal, some days you just wanna write your thoughts, and some days a story. This gives me the chance to allow others to connect to my lyrics to maybe something similar they are going through, or have experienced, without my anxiety getting the best of me. Maybe I could motivate others to also not be afraid to take a risk, and follow the music beats in their hearts, just like artists have done for me.

I had my life figured out, and thought I knew exactly what I wanted, and how I was going to get there. God had a different plan for my journey. He stepped in, took the wheel, and re-routed me to where I should be goin'. He put that destination inside me a long time ago - I just needed to turn on my GPS...

This is the soundtrack to my road trip.

"This Chicago Girl"

I grew up in the middle of a block
In a small raised ranch
Neighbors comin' out yellin' – "Get off my grass!"
Oh how we laughed

Little league playin' at Hiawatha Park
Football, Bocce Ball
Our summer landmark

The Grand Avenue train always stoppin' traffic
People honkin' their horns like it mattered
Yellin' and swearin' over the rail clatter

Saturday mornin' sittin' on the front stoop
Talkin' to my girlfriends
Plannin' our night out in the Loop
Attended all-girl Catholic high school
Always sneakin' into the all-boys right next to

No matter what direction the wind blows
Your wind will always carry me home
When life throws me into a whirl
It can't pull these roots out of
This Chicago girl

Hoppin' the bus to Wrigley Field every weekend
Wearin' that Cubbie Blue with that
Old Style drinkin'

I was raised by Frankie, Bobby, and Deano
Singin' along to the radio
Headin' downtown on Superior for a slice
And North Avenue for Italian Ice

Headed to the candy store
At the end of the block
On our speed bikes and roller blades
Wearin' Mary Jane's and cuffed socks
Air Heads, Swedish Fish, Fun Dip
Made our day
Only a dollar went a long way

At fifteen, I learned how to parallel park
Had to be home when the street lights came on
Before dark

A day at Brookfield Zoo - my favorite place
The museums, aquarium
And Millennium Park off the lake
Standin' in a glass box
Off the edge of the Willis Tower
And the look on my face
When my stomach goes sour

Navy Pier and all its beauty
Late night cruises, the Ferris wheel
And a 3D movie

China Town, Greek Town, and Little Italy
Known as the Second and Windy City
Michigan Avenue shinin' bright
Wavin' that flag
Of the red stars and blue stripes

Stayin' home from school with the winter snow
Took our sleds to the hill and let 'em go

Daddy worked all night on the plow
Sometimes wouldn't come home for days now
Wishin' the storm would end somehow

I wrote him letters
Inside the bag lunch I made
I miss you Daddy.
Goodnight - drive safe.
I really wish you stayed.

"Can't Count the Sheep"

Birds out my window
Sittin' in a tree
Singin' that tune that's oh so sweet
Stars shinin' bright with a twinkle in the sky
The manmade lake lookin' back at the moonlight

Layin' in bed lookin' up at the clouds
Seems so peaceful, but yet so loud
Eyes wide open, but closed inside
The press on my chest and tears in my eyes
And nobody layin' next to me sayin'
It'll be alright

When life gets heavy, always on the go
Nobody by your side, just you and the road
Just tryin' to figure it all out
What's under your feet
Findin' that balance between love
And chasin' your dreams

I thank God at night
For blessing me with this life
And ask Him to calm the noise as I try to sleep
Sometimes those thoughts get so loud
Can't count the sheep

Reflections appear crystal clear
Just like a mirror
Thinkin' what my life would be like
If you were still here

Life gave you lemons
And threw me a lime
Drinkin' your lemonade
With a twist in mine

This drink meant for me ain't for the weak
Sippin' slow, on the go
No vino or whiskey
Agin' with wisdom
Improves with time
Yours went sour
While mine still shines

This journey I'm on
No matter how fast or how slow
Will lead me one day
To where I'm supposed to go
The noise will clear in my head
And share all my dreams with you next to me
Lyin' in bed
The love that is lost, found in your eyes
With the strength to drink from my cup
With a lime

Under the stars we lay down to sleep
I find that twinkle in your heart
Can't count the sheep

"Turned the Other Cheek"

I've always been told
If you don't talk about it
It will just go away
Don't ask, don't speak, don't repeat
It's just the way it is
It's nobody's business
Keep the peace and let it be
You'll let down our family

I did what I was told
Wore my heart on my sleeve
Gave everything I had
Money, clothes, the shoes off my feet
To make everyone happy

Put my feelings aside and put up a wall
Shadowed it with a smile and stood tall
Always just one call or text away, and I was there
Not because I had to
Because that's what you do
When you truly care

The time had come when I needed you
Only to find out that you were untrue
You traded my weakness for your strength
Used my hand to slap my face
I craved your love that made my heart leak
I needed you the most and you
Turned the other cheek

It's not my place
To point out what you did wrong
You see, God blessed me to write this song
In the end it's the choices we make
And excuses we break
That defines the journey we lead
I forgive you
This is me
Keeping my peace

I have no regrets of how I was led
The hurt, the pain, the memories in my head
This path has brought me to where I am today
A beautiful life, a heart of gold
More than you could say

So if you're thinkin' of reachin' out
I won't ask, won't speak, won't repeat
This is me
Turnin' the other cheek

"1-55"

Ever since I was a little girl
Music has always been a part of my world
Never was an AM kinda chick
In the car blastin' that FM station
Doesn't matter - you pick

In my room with the turned up boombox
Singin' and dancin' in my pj's
With the windows open
And the door locked

In grammar school I started in the church choir
Sang with Sister Marie
In C minor
Music major in high school
Somethin' always in my heart
But never pursued

I sang solo, "I Hope You Dance"
By Leeann Womack on stage
In front of my class
Rememberin' the standing ovation
That filled up my cup
I walked out of the theater
No one showed up

That was the last time I sang on stage
Or in front of people to this day
Anxiety kicks in and nerves take over
Overthinkin' and second guessin'
What I can cover

There's only one place I belt out and sing
When I get in my car and take a drive
Windows rolled down
On I-55

Just me and the highway headin' south
Through Illinois cornfields and small towns
Gets me excited and feelin' free
Lettin' out that side of me

No one around puttin' in their two cents
Sayin' what is and isn't meant
Just the music inside me
That makes me smile and so happy

Who knows, one day
You might see me or my music
On the radio or on stage
Inspiring all to keep chasin' dreams
In your own special way
Until then, you can catch me
On the Illinois highway
Turnin' the page

"February 29"

Every four years
There's this random day in February
That pops out of nowhere
And often unnoticed by many

Three hundred and sixty-six
Instead of three sixty-five
I dedicate this day to why I'm alive
Born with additional love in my veins
Sometimes takes me a minute
To remember my age

I celebrated my Sweet Sixteen
When I turned four years old
I look pretty good for my age - so I'm told
Guys always sayin', they like 'em young
When I turn eighty-four, I'll be twenty-one

Born with a forever young heart deep inside
Graduated beauty school when I was five

Some might call it a gift
Others will say it's just a myth
How could someone not have a birthday
And only when the Olympics play

Well, I like to think that
On Leap Day when the earth shifts
The stars aligned and gravity stepped in
Catch my drift

So you see, I'm not the only one
Who was born by the stars
Not by Venus or by Mars
We carry two birthstones
How unique is that
Amethyst, and Aquamarine for the years
It doesn't come back

It might seem strange and a little weird
But life would be boring
Without Leap Year
February 29 is not supernatural or tarot
Just an extra day shot by Cupid's Arrow

So if you meet someone
Who was born on this day
Don't call them names and turn away
Keep them close to you for a long time
You'll be forever young in your heart
Just like mine

To all the Leap Year babies
Let's celebrate
I share this special day with you
Happy Birthday

"Anthony"

What can I say - it's been a long time
Way back when things were fine
Comin' to visit you on the weekends
At your city apartment
But it would depend
If a game was playin' there off Clark
Good luck tryin' to park
Back when Uber wasn't a thing
Sometimes had to park six blocks
Off Irving

Then I moved away and times changed
Life took a turn and it wasn't the same
Distance grew between us from all the drama
Comin' from both ends of Daddy and Momma

Their problems tore us apart
Put us in the middle
And left with a broken heart

I wish you had the strength to walk away
Instead kept it in and sent it my way
The cycle repeated and caused me to stray

That wasn't the life
I was put on this earth to live
Yellin', cryin', jealously, and competition

Life is too short for it to pass us by
From the choices people make
Even in our own bloodline

Problems are common in families
When it hurts the ones you love
And tears them apart
It's how you move forward
Through the goodness of your heart

I wish things were different between you and I
Missin' your face and wonderin' why
Rememberin' the good times
When we were kids
Always laughin', teasin', and all the digs

Even though we were different
In our special way
We shared the same friends, school,
Even work at one point, you could say
Sometimes fight like cats and dogs
Then got over it, and carried on

You always protected me
I looked out for you from the start
Even though only just a year apart

As each day goes by
Wonderin' what you're like at this age
If you're single, married, or engaged

Hopin' and prayin' you're healthy and happy
Even if it means
Livin' this life without me
You will always be my best friend
My Brother
Anthony

"Ain't Got Nothin'
On a Hairdresser"

Jump in the car early in the mornin'
Headed to the salon yawnin'
Gotta stop for a Venti on the way
Full book ahead on a Saturday

Sometimes behind the chair
Ten hours or more covered in hair
Hustlin' for the cheeks in the seats
Haven't sat down, eaten, or even peed
Inhalin' all the smells
Chemicals, aerosols, and God knows what else

Hairdressers are up with the sun
Bartenders start when the day is done
Yea, you have your Happy Hour regulars
Drownin' their sorrows over a drink
But it don't beat the ladies sittin'
And spillin' all the tea

No more or lesser
Sorry bartender
But you ain't got nothin' on a hairdresser

First client walks in fifteen minutes late
Has hair down to her rear
Covered in gel and hair spray
Scheduled for a style or an up-do
Tryin' to squeeze in a last minute shampoo

Finally finished just in time
Just when she says she changed her mind
Instead of her hair up, she wants it down
And here walks in your next client now

No more or lesser
Sorry bartender
But you ain't got nothin' on a hairdresser

Sunday afternoon after church and brunch
Ladies walk in on a time crunch
Here for their weekly wash and set
Teased high to the sky with Aqua Net
Goin' on and on about their husbands
Lazy and good for nothin'
Askin' you why you're still single
If you wanna go out with their son
Or how 'bout Christian Mingle

Hair looks great and dressed to the nine
Puts in your hand
A piece of hard candy, and a dime

No more or lesser
Sorry bartender
But you ain't got nothin' on a hairdresser

But there is one thing we both could say
Y'all share with us your DNA
Whether it's on a glass or on the floor
We always take it all in
And leave it at the door

We ain't no doctor or a shrink
But just think
You spend most of your time with us anyway
While we work off tips, commission,
Or an hourly rate
We don't write prescriptions
Or take your insurance
And won't send you an extra bill
For our service

Ok bartender, so maybe it's true
Maybe hairdressers got nothin' on you
We do share that special link
And what can I say
At the end of a long day
Hairdressers go out for a nice hard drink

By the time we leave your hair will turn gray
Your cheeks will then sit in our seats
And watch us slay
So whether we are at the bar or the beauty shop
One thing is certain
Money well spent
And pretty awesome jobs

"My Little Guy"

I brought you home at ten weeks old
You pressed your paw against the glass
And caught my eye when I walked past
Lookin' at me with those big eyes
One ear up flapped over
And the other standin' high
They carried you out and brought you to me
That was the moment I knew
I was meant to be your mommy

You give the true meaning of number one fan
Makin' it all worth it with your paw in my hand
That excited feelin' when I come home
Seein' your face holdin' a bone
Can't wait to go for a walk outside
Or in the car for a ride

You're always by my side
I won't ever let this life pass you by
Here's to you
My little guy

There were rough times when you got sick
Bladder stones, surgeries, tumors, and cysts
Your little heart murmur is still beatin' strong
All the prescription medicines and food
And you still move along
Nothin' ever gets in your way
You're my inspiration each and every day

Now fourteen years old and not a day shy
You're not by my side
I will never let this life pass you by
Here's to you
My little guy

You and I together livin' this crazy life
Through the good and the bad
The happy times and sad

One thing's for sure
A dog's love is the most pure
I am so blessed to share this ride with you
And will always be here until the day comes
Where you can't pull through

Holdin' your paw tight with tears in my eyes
I will always be right by your side
Here's to you
My little guy

And in case you didn't know
My little guy's name is
Pacino

"Title Wasn't Earned"

Ever since I was a little girl
I dreamt of the day
Of whom I would share my heart with
And my world
Just the two of us in this life together
Makin' memories and creating a future
For the better
Knowin' that we would be together forever

It was a rainy day in the middle of spring
When I walked down the aisle
And put on your ring
I said I do with all the love in my heart
At our fairy tale wedding
And a life I couldn't wait to start

I gave you all of me
With eyes only for you
With your eyes lookin' back at me
That were untrue
Standin' by and sacrificing to be a good wife
To make you happy and everyone in your life

Not even a year
You left me with eyes full of tears
Tryin' to understand what I had learned
The only thing you had committed to
Was a title that wasn't earned

I hope she makes you happy
And you provide her with a life
That is full of true love
And not a lie
When you look into her eyes
I hope you show her that you truly care
Along with the children you both have bared

I have no resentment of ever knowing you
Even the struggle, heartbreak
And pain you put me through

Everything in life happens for a reason
And I thank God every day
For blessing me with your treason
I would have continued to live a life
That wasn't meant for me
And close my eyes for the sanctity

If it wasn't for you
I wouldn't be livin' this beautiful life I now live
So thank you, I hope it was all worth it

Everything in our past
Is now nothin' but ash
Those memories have burned
The only thing you left me with
Is a title that wasn't earned

"It's the Little Things"

Some things in life were meant to stay
And some things just go away
Lookin' up at the sky
And always askin' God why

We pray for things we cannot see
And want more than what's in front of me
But sometimes we lose sight
And it's never enough
With the things we thought made us happy
And yet, life is still tough

It's the little things in life that make me happy
They put the value in the bigger things
And what can be
The bigger things then seem more like a gift
Rather than a void we keep tryin' to lift

If we forget about those little things
We'll never be satisfied
And the things we keep wantin' more of
Get thrown to the wayside
Always with a mindset of wantin' bigger and better
But it's the little things
That holds it all together

Money, cars, the Botox in our face
Mask the things that could never be replaced
The lines and scars that tell a story
The little things that make up you
And all your glory

So when life gets too fast
And you try to keep up
Take a look inside your drinking cup
Is it half full or half empty
Or maybe overflowin' the edge with envy

Instead of always tryin' to stay above
Take a step back
And look at what the cup is made of

It's the little things in life
That makes me smile
It's the little things
That makes it all worthwhile

"From The South"

Now, I know what y'all are thinkin'
What does a girl with a background from Italy
Know anything about the South or Country
Well, allow me to explain
How the differences are actually
More the same

Our ancestors came from nothin'
Workin' every day in the field bright and early
To put food on the table for their family
If you have ever been to Italy and looked around
It's surrounded by beautiful country
With landscaped grounds

We love our barrels
As they sit and ferment
Your Mason jars tapped with moonshine
And our glasses held high
With rose', white, or red wine
Taken a load off
And havin' a good time

Now one thing's certain
We got us some good eatin'
Y'all pluck your chickens
We hang our salami from the ceilin'
All the greens, no matter how leafy
Mustard, collard, or rapini

We can fry anything - you name it
Chicken, steak, zucchini, or calamari
We even have great taste in cars
Ford and Ferrari

Romance fills up our hearts
Sittin' under a tree watchin' the fireflies
Or down a canal on a gondola ride
Sharing the moonlight from both sides

There is one thing I will share
You see, my family is from southern Italy
It's a bit different there
The northerners are like the Yankees
They eat pasta sauce unlike our gravy
Yours is white over warm biscuits
Ours is red over pasta dishes

So you see we are both from The South
And pretty much the same
Just with a different soundin' last name
Both have accents, just different roots
Oh, and in case you didn't notice
Italy is shaped
Like a cowboy boot

"Lee"

Back when I was a teenager, some time ago
I volunteered at this nursing home
Would go and help out on my spare time
Sometimes spend the whole day
And wouldn't mind

We would sit inside and sing together
Or on a bench outside and enjoy the weather
Knowin' by tomorrow
They wouldn't remember

It was dinner time and they would gather 'round
As they grab my arm to help them sit down
A voice yelled out - Hey Lee
I didn't realize he was talkin' to me
Just wanted a refill on his coffee

I was confused and couldn't understand
Why he called me Lee and was so blunt
Then I realized my sweatshirt said
Lee Jeans on the front
White with Lee in big blue letters
And then later became my name to all the others

There was this sweet lady, Mary
Who would just sit and cry
Wonderin' why her family never came by
Lookin' out the window
Is where she would stay
Only come to find out
They were here yesterday

I grabbed a tissue
Wiped the tears from her sorrow
And promised her they would be here tomorrow
I knew that tomorrow was unforeseen
So I went home
Threw my sweatshirt in the wash
And always made sure it was clean

Even if they couldn't remember
That sweatshirt was my small gesture
And hearin' them yell out - Hey Lee
Will always be in my memory

"Scared to Love You"

He said I can give you the world
I want you to be my girl
You make me so happy
Can you see yourself to be with me

I know he's not him
I know he's not the rest of them
I know I'm not that naive girl that used to be
I know I deserve to be happy

So why do I push you away
Put up a wall and won't say
All the things I keep inside
Feelin' and emotion that I hide

Are you the kind of man
Who will listen and understand
Will you be there for awhile
Take the time to go the extra mile
Or are you here for the moment
Get what you can to get noticed

How will I know when to unleash my heart again
How will I know you're the one that can mend
How will I know I'm not wastin' my time
How will I know if you're mine

My heart has been healin' from black and blue
My heart is scared to love you

He said I can buy you fancy things
Travel anywhere and give you everything
I can make your worries seem so small
Take care of you and do it all

But behind all that what's inside
Do you have a heart that you hide
Can you open up to mine
And be able to put the money aside
To know if you're truly mine

How will I know when it's right
How will I know to shine in your light
How will I know if you're sincere
How will I know to let go of the fear

My heart has been healin' from black and blue
My heart is scared to love you

"Hey Jesus"

New neighbor moved in downstairs
Loud and obnoxious
Wanna pull out my hair

Smells like fried chicken
And Cheech and Chong
I just decorated outside for the spring
She opened her door
And there goes her dog
Went right up to my Easter egg
And then right there, lifted his leg

Hey Jesus -
If you're lookin' down from up there
Maybe you could give me a hand over here
Hey Jesus

Took a drive down 47 on this beautiful day
Goin' apple pickin' at the farm
After church on a Sunday
Got to the orchard to grab my first one
Then out of nowhere, I got stung

Hey Jesus -
If you're lookin' down from up there
Maybe you could give me a hand over here
Hey Jesus

Sun is shinin' bright
With the windows down and the wind in my hair
Headin' nowhere
Just soakin' it up
The car in front of me swerved and hit a truck
My tire blew and I yelled....

Hey Jesus -
If you're lookin' down from up there
Maybe you could give me a hand over here
Hey Jesus

Went to a concert on a rainy day
To see my favorite singer for the first time
Over two hours away
Stood in line with boots on my feet
To see if I would be so lucky
To get my first meet and greet

As I got closer it started to look promising
Handin' them out
To the few people in front of me
With butterflies in my stomach, I was next
Sorry darlin', we ain't got none left

Hey Jesus -
If you're lookin' down from up there
Maybe you could give me a hand over here
Hey Jesus

Stayin' in and catchin' up on laundry
Threw a load in and turned it to cold
Cycle was over and to my surprise
Cold turned hot and I almost died
The machine broke and shrunk all my clothes

Hey Jesus -
If you're lookin' down from up there
Maybe you could give me a hand over here
Hey Jesus

Unloaded the groceries from my car
To get to my door I have to walk
Down the sidewalk and through the courtyard
Right before I got to my place
The bottom fell out, and there goes my eggs
All down my legs

Hey Jesus -
If you're lookin' down from up there
Maybe you could give me a hand over here
Hey Jesus

"It Just Didn't Fit"

I see you lookin' my way
Starin' at me with that handsome face
A tall drink restin' in my hand
Gettin' lost and makin' plans

Those long summer walks lookin' in your eyes
Cozied up on the coach late at night
Gettin' lost in the moments you never forget
But then I stepped back and looked right in

My wheel went left, yours went right
Drivin' with all that baggage was a little tight
I wanna hit the road until we hit sand
We detoured on the way in your mini van

No matter how fun the ride between you and I
It's not just you in the passenger side
Windows rolled down
Listenin' to Brett and Thomas Rhett
Turned into Disney's Greatest Hits
That's when I knew
It just didn't fit

Now don't get me wrong
I long for the day
I get to carry that pink and blue baggage
Along the way
Goin' to baseball games and ballet
Openin' a card drawn with crayon
On Mother's Day

But when I look at you and you see me
All I can see is you, plus three
Not one the same, neither with me

As much as I tried to make it work
And carried it on for a bit
It just didn't fit

"Let Me Be Your Whiskey"

Starin' at that glass
Half full or half empty
Drownin' your sorrows
In a would that's hefty

Turnin' to your friends - Jack and Jim
To get you through the hard times
When things get grim
They will blur out your problems
And wash them away
They're good for one night, but never stay
Leavin' you with tomorrow in more pain

Give me a drink from your cup
And everything you pour in that fills you up
Embrace all the things that get you drunk
I wanna be the one who gets you tipsy
Slide your glass in my hand
Let me be your whiskey

Take a shot and celebrate
Somethin' special headed your way
Or livin' it up at a party
With your name written in a Sharpie
Livin' in the moment as life passes by
Buildin' the excitement with a high
Tomorrow wanna do it all again
Or at least until the hangover ends

Give me a drink from your cup
And everything you pour in that fills you up
Embrace all the things that get you drunk
I wanna be the one who gets you tipsy
Slide your glass in my hand
Let me be your whiskey

Share all the things that get you dizzy
Good, bad, and ugly
Pour me your whiskey

"What's Meant for You
Will Find You"

They always say
Stop lookin' he'll come your way
Then when you stop lookin'
And go out just to mingle
They start askin'
Why you still single

Online dating is a disaster
Catfish, cheaters
And guys with one thing they're after
Blind dates ain't no fun
Turn back around and just run

Then there's church to meet that nice guy
Maybe God will give you a sign
Singin' to the heavens above
Standin' in a pew
Someone turns to you and says
Peace be with you
Holds your hand for a long time
About 30 years older and winks his eye
You kneel and thank God for the sign
That I may be single for a long time

So don't worry if you haven't found the one
They're out there somewhere
And that day will come
You will meet that special person
When it's due
You can always look but
What's meant for you will find you

The grocery store is always a good time
Wonderin' what you could find
Standin' up by the produce
You notice a guy
He's lookin' over at you
Squeezin' a melon tryin' to picture you nude
Winkin' his eye with a giant smirk
Comin' right outta the woodwork

Let's not forget those bar nights
Sittin' next to a table candle light
Someone buys you a drink
Chats up some small talk
Asks for your number
Wants to take you home and get you drunker

The dating world is all a game
After a while it's just the same
Tryin' to look for somethin' we think we want
Just to always end up in the wrong spot

So just go out and have fun
And don't worry if you haven't found the one
They are out there somewhere
And that day will come
You will meet that special person when it's due
You can always look but
What's meant for you will find you

"11/7"

When I was young
I always knew what I wanted to do
Be a hairdresser and apply makeup too
I would play beauty shop
And cut the hair off my Barbie
Then play dress up to an imaginary party

On the playground
I'd braid my friends' hair
And when I was a teenager
I bought my own chair
Brought all my friends over in my basement
Startin' my own little business
Makin' a statement
There was nothin' in this world
That made me as happy
Then helpin' people feel good
And look pretty

Then one day I was drivin' to work
Comin' to an intersection on a green light
A car came out of nowhere
From the opposite side
Ran the red and hit me head on
My car was totaled
A 2-door Tiburon
I blacked out and lost feelin' in my arm
The fire department came
And pulled me from harm

I remember this moment like it was yesterday
Layin' in an emergency room
Hooked up to machines
With a given diagnosis that was unforeseen
The doctor said you need surgery
Everything in my wrist had been ripped apart
Layin' there with a broken heart
They weren't sure of the outcome
Due to the amount of damage
Everything was completely numb

The surgeon asked what I did for work
I told him I do hair
He said, I'm so sorry dear
I know this isn't fair
But you will have to find a new career

And just like that my dream was crushed
But that didn't stop me
I never gave up
Pushed hard and made it through
To get the most out of what I can do

Even though all of this altered my plans
I knew it was all in God's hands
My right wrist was the only thing that interfered
With the path I chose for myself
In that career
If that car accident never happened
I would have abandoned my other talents
And what I imagined

This day changed my life
From the blessings I was given
A beautiful tragedy
On 11/7

"Oswego"

Lived in this town for a while now
In my cute little apartment
Decorated like a farmhouse
With a cozy balcony facing the courtyard
And a cherry blossom tree
For my scenery
A sweet little place just for me

Peaceful walks around the lake
Surrounded by willow trees, ducks and geese
People out fishin' knee deep
Couples on a bench kissin'
Watchin' the sunset and the water glisten

This prairie Midwest town
Sure ain't like the city
Rows of corn, off of Route 34
In the middle of Kendall County

That skyline's not so far away
Leadin' me back to Chicago
But there's no place like my Illinois home
In Oswego

Headin' down Main Street in the heart of town
Remembered for all the muscle cars
And drag strip racin'
With people from all around
All the way back to 1955 to 79
It's been a while now

Kayaking on the Fox River
Summer concerts in the park
And a Christmas Walk in the winter
Residents are so warm and friendly
Always havin' a good time
At the local brewery

You can get everything homemade
At the ma and pop shops
From antiques to spices
To donuts, cheesecake, coffee and tea
Or head to the Farm N' Fleet off Route 30
Next door in Montgomery

Even though I left behind
My city roots in Chicago
The prairie opened up my Midwestern heart
To a home in a town called Oswego

"Ginger"

Your strawberry blonde hair and light eyes
Not a day went by
Where he wasn't by your side

Held your hand everywhere
Sway you around like Fred Astaire
In the kitchen or in public
He didn't care
Just as long as you were there

Always out and dressed to the nine
Your outfits matched in your own design
Sharin' glasses of fine red wine
In Italian, he'd call you mine

He built everything with his hands
Provided for you as your man
Snow white hair with a tan
He called you Ginger
Your number one fan

'Til this day
I'll always remember
How he looked at you that way
Hopin' I would have that one day

He called you Ginger
With love in his eyes
He called you Ginger
Until he died

The day came when he said goodbye
Cancer took him to the sky
When he left, he took your mind
And all the memories left behind

He called you Ginger
You forgotten mine
He called you Ginger
'Til you met him in the sky

"Dream Catcher"
(A Lullaby)

Follow a shooting star
Make a wish from afar
Gaze upon the midnight skylight
Right before you say goodnight

Get lost in all the things
Fly high and spread your wings
Starry night and moonbeams
Sleep tight and chase your dreams

Close your eyes and sleep
Rest your head down in peace
Breathe in your day
And send it God's way
Thank Him for each breath He gave
Let go of all your struggles and pray

Hangin' there up on the wall
I glance at you come nightfall
Reminder of what's outside
Will all subside when I close my eyes
Get lost in all the things that matter
Sweet dreams beautiful dream catcher

"Butterflies"

I see you across the room
Standin' in the night
A country bar, a band playin'
Under string lights

You're with your boys drinkin' whiskey
Havin' a good time
You look my way
And I get locked on your baby blues
Sittin' on a high top with my girlfriends
Sippin' on a Blue Moon

That handsome face
Is given me such a high
Baby, I got those butterflies

That feelin' that you get
That turns on your insides
Can't think straight
Can't wait
Just want you by my side
When you press up against my lips
My stomach does a flip
Baby, take me to the sky
Givin' me those butterflies

Goin' out, first date
Wanna look perfect
Can't be late
Waitin' for that moment
When you first see him that night
All cleaned up
Lookin so sharp
Turnin' up the Fahrenheit
Baby, you got me hypnotized
Givin' me those butterflies

Lightin' up my phone throughout the day
With messages and texts just to say
On the other side missin' your face
Hearin' from you is like winnin' a prize
Givin' me every time
Those butterflies

"Ever Wonder"

Ever wonder
What it'll be like when you're eighty-five
Old and grey
And if you're still alive

Ever wonder what life was like back then
When your grandparents were your age
Way back when

Ever wonder if they lived a similar life
Just in a different year
Way before your time

Ever wonder if it's all just a cycle
Same patterns
Just a new way of survival

Ever wonder what it would be like
If we never had to say goodbye

Ever wonder what you'd say
If they were here with you today
Ever wonder what they look like
As they look down on you
From way up high
Ever wonder if they're proud
Of all the things you're doin' now

Ever wonder what you'd say
If they were here with you today

Ever wonder where you'd go
Maybe dinner and a show
Ever wonder what they'd think
Maybe take'em for a drink
Ever wonder what they're like
If they act like you
And have your eyes

Ever wonder what you'd say
If they were here with you today

Ever wonder if they're here
If they're that voice in your ear
Ever wonder what they could see
If they're that cardinal in the tree
Ever wonder if they're sendin' you light
When you look up at the stars
Late at night

Ever wonder what you'd say
If they were here with you today

"Coconut"

At the beach
On a blanket in the sand
White painted toes
Gettin' a tan
A frozen Pina Colada in my hand
There ain't nothin' better
Under the sun in warm weather

Sip it up slow
Under an umbrella, layin low
Soakin' up the tropical breeze
Hot pink bikini by the sea
Fresh pineapple just cut
Getting' buzzed off that coconut

Swim up bar
Background playin' that four stringed guitar
A flower in my hair
Bronze skin, feet bare
Under a blue sky
Given me such a high

Wanna come play in the sand
Walk along the beach
And hold my hand
Cool off and take a dip
Get a drink and take a sip
Come with me let's have a party
I'll share with you my Bacardi

Sip it slow
Under an umbrella, layin' low
Soakin' up the tropical breeze
Hot pink bikini by the sea
Fresh pineapple just cut
Getting' buzzed off that coconut

"Your Frosting"

Baby my sugar intake ain't right
Doctors can't control it
It's you given me that frostbite
I don't want those candles on my birthday
It's that whip cream that's drivin' me crazy

When you press those lips against mine
Your sugar is given me such a high
I want that cake and eat it too
Baby, my sweet tooth's just for you

Come give me that candy rush
Move in close with that sweet touch
Your ingredients come with a warning
Baby, ain't no diet restrictions for your frosting

Givin' me the shakes when you walk by
Can't control the hyper on the inside
Or what your doin' to me physically
You got me like a kid askin' for candy
Baby, you're givin' me a cavity

Come on baby let's get together and bake
All your toppings and fillings
Just think of what we can make
But you know what's got me smiling

When you press those lips against mine
Your sugar is given me such a high
I want that cake and eat it too
Baby, my sweet tooth's just for you

Come give me that candy rush
Move in close with that sweet touch
Your ingredients come with a warning
Baby, ain't no diet restrictions for your frosting

"Smartphone"

New fad, gotta have
Download that new app
Facebook, Instagram
Twitter, Snap Chat

New pic, gotta tag
Send a Poke or a Tweet
Click Like on your feed
Change your face, young or old
Choose a filter, Selfie Mode
Set location - Where you at?
Where you goin' - Google Map

Hey phone - You think you're smart
One thing you ain't got, is a heart
Can't reproduce, gotta upgrade you
Your screen ain't the real thing
Gotta answer when you ring
All that noise can corrupt
But I can always turn you off
And never forget
To just look up

Facetime, far away
Watch a video, play a game
Send a text, or a call
DM message, or on your wall
Email, voicemail
Shop online for a sale
Pay a bill, send cash
Uber Eats, Door Dash
Password for everything
Pop socket or a ring

Hey phone - You think you're smart
One thing you ain't got, is a heart
Can't reproduce, gotta upgrade you
Your screen ain't the real thing
Gotta answer when you ring
All that noise can corrupt
But I can always turn you off
And never forget
To just look up

"Don't Want Your Cannoli"

Growin' up as an Italian girl
People automatically assume
They know who rocks my world

They want to set me up with
Their sons, nephews, or cousins for a date
Just because that blood
Runs through my veins
Doesn't mean we have the same taste

Because I'm Italian
You may think you know me
Sorry Vito, Rocco, and Vinny
Don't want your cannoli

I've been down that road before
Just not for me
It reminds me of dating my family
I'm not typical, I step outside the box
You can enjoy your tall glass of Limon cello
While I have my Tennessee whiskey
On the rocks

Now don't get me wrong
There are some handsome Italian men out there
But I prefer that southern drawl
With blue eyes and lighter hair

I can't speak for all Italian girls
That's just me
Sorry Paisan
Don't want your cannoli

Thinkin' that tradition was the only option
But as I got older
I looked deep into my heart
And found out what it truly wants
Because life is too short
Sometimes you need a fresh start

One day I'll find my glass of whiskey
That'll warm my heart
And the Italian within me
But until then, I'm sorry to say
Arrivederci to Vito, Rocco, and Vinny
Don't want your cannoli

"When Nothin' Goes Right – Go Left"

When the sun ain't shinin' and the sky looks grey
When the work keeps draggin' and it's been a long day
When the check-out line is twenty minutes long
When you turn on the radio and hear a sad song
When life's got you down, not feelin' your best
When nothin' goes right - go left

Turn that frown upsidown
Find the happy in your worry
Don't cry, keep your head held high
When you're afraid, look the other way
Where there's love, you'll rise above
Life's too short to be stressed
When nothin' goes right - go left

When you have a deadline that you can't make
When you haven't slept and your body aches
When your alarm didn't go off and you're runnin' late
When you're on empty and haven't ate
When everything around you puts a pain in your chest
When nothin' goes right - go left

Turn that frown upsidown
Find the happy in your worry
Don't cry, keep your head held high
When you're afraid, look the other way
Where there's love, you'll rise above
Life's too short to be stressed
When nothin' goes right - go left

When you get to that fork in the road
When you can't decide which way to go
When you have to choose between what's right or wrong
When you try to find where you belong
When you choose you, and pass that test
When nothing goes right - always go left

"Here's to the Single Girl"

Here's to the girl workin' 9 to 5
Here's to the girl workin' overtime
Here's to the girl who lives alone
Here's to the girl who still lives at home

No one to help out with the rent
Tryin' to manage every cent
No Valentine or date to the dance
A pretty face with no romance

A single mom tryin' to balance a little mouth to feed
Work and school
Tryin' to succeed
And still takes care and feels good
Regardless of the comments
Being misunderstood

Here's to the girl who keeps her head high
Here's to the girl who owns her own drive
Here's to the girl who has no fears
Here's to the girl who wipes her own tears
Here's to the girl who carries the weight of the world
Here's to the single girl

Here's to the girl who has loved and lost
Tackled every challenge she's crossed
Here's to the girl who's been done wrong
Battled her feelin's and moved along
Here's to the girl who travels alone
Lives in the moment and enjoys every milestone

No hand to hold under the stars
No call or text askin' where you are
No one to kiss her goodnight
No one to tell her it will be alright

Single girls have a fire inside
They'll keep goin'
Never run and hide
A strength that could never compare
A mother, manager, student or athlete
A soldier, nurse, waitress, or millionaire
Just to name a few
Single girl - Here's to you

"Nina"

Sweet pea
My mini me
Beautiful out and in
Never holds back
Always determined

A giant heart
Extremely smart
Light up a room when you smile
Your sense of humor
And your style

I'll always be someone you could look up to
Listen and guide you through
Even when I'm not there with you
I'll be by your side
Good, bad, or when you cry
When the world gets heavy for you to hold
Think of me as you grow old
Just know
I'll never let go

You inspire me everyday
Your beauty and your strength
At such a young age
I can't wait to see where life takes you
And all the amazing things you do
You're like my tattoo
I will always love you

There's not a day that goes by I can't wait to see ya
My cousin
Nina

"This Ain't No Drive-thru"

Hey ladies, this one's for you
Y'all know that guy
Tryin' to make his move
Drivin' along in his car
Pulls down the window
And yells from afar
Whistlin' and hollerin'
Like he's orderin' from a menu
Boy keep drivin'
This ain't no drive-thru

Sorry we ain't servin'
What you're cravin'
A midnight snack
No side of fries
For your Big Mac
Ain't no happy meal
Made your way
This Dairy Queen is closed
For this milk shake
My menu ain't for you
Boy keep drivin'
This ain't no drive-thru

At the bar
Someone ordered you a drink
You look over
He gives you a wink
The waitress comes back over
And in her hand
Slips you a napkin
From that man
It says -
Hey sexy, wanna get outta here
Your place or mine
As he drinks his beer
You start to write
I sure do
My place, but not with you
Boy, keep drinkin'
This ain't no drive-thru

Sorry we ain't servin'
What your cravin'
A hard drink til mornin'
Ain't got no chaser
For your Captain Morgan
No cocktail
Stirred or shaken
This bar is dry
For what I'm sippin'
This happy hour ain't for you
Boy, keep drinkin'
This ain't no drive-thru

"Superman"

A hero
Fights our battles
When we cry
Someone we long for
To help us by
The strength we desire
To save our life
And keep us safe
From our fears inside

A handsome glow
Body of steel
A champion with sex appeal
Built under a cape
Rescuing girls to escape

Superman you're a dream
To every girl and every boy
Spreadin' hope and courage
Of what could be
Boys wanna be you
Girls wanna be with you
An icon everyone lives up to

But Superman, how 'bout you
What's underneath all that blue
Behind the steel what's inside
Clark Kent, why do you hide

You are beautiful
Glasses and all
You don't need to put up a wall
For you are the one who is real
Superman is based on how you feel
That is the dream of what is meant
There'd be no Superman
Without Clark Kent

"Two Rocking Chairs"

On a porch sit two rocking chairs
Next to each other in a pair
Vintage and handmade
Sway back and forth under the shade

The wood is stressed and a little worn
Barrin' the sun, rain, and the storms
Still peacefully rock and sway
As they rest upon each day

The stretch marks tell a story
How they carry on in all their glory
The peace they give from one another
And the love shared between each other

In time there will come a day
The two rocking chairs will wear away
And slowly begin to lose their sway
The history left behind their pieces
Will remain on that porch with the seasons

Two rocking chairs that sway together
On a porch filled with memories
That last forever

"Never Been Fishin'"

A girl that has grown up
In that city livin'
Had everything around me
Catchin' cabs
And fast pace walkin'
Restaurants and take-out
If I got hungry
Walk to the corner
For mornin' coffee
Headed to the lake
For some summer beachin'
Sorry y'all
Hate to admit it, but
Never been fishin'

Anyone out there
That wants to teach me
I know what you're thinkin'
That's crazy
I didn't grow up in camouflage
Only city alleys
With a parking garage
You could say
I'm a different breed
I guess that's the country
Tucked away in me
So put those arms around this girl
And show me what I've been missin'
Makin' me blush
Never been fishin'

Ain't familiar with a fishin' pole
How to line
Or how to hold
Know nothin' bout fishin' bait
The difference between
Real and fake
What to do if I get a bite
If I fall in
Would you take a dive

Wanna be that guy
Show me what I've been wishin'
Sittin' by the water kissin'
Never been fishin'

"How Does It Taste"

Hey there heartbreaker
How ya doin'
Lookin' different now
I see your hair's been losin'
Not so fit
Let yourself go
Funny how that's all that mattered to you
Some time ago

Nice car
No more drop top
Showin' off round the city
I guess that drive died
Lookin' a little rusty

It's funny how life takes a turn
And comes back to you
With a burn
Thinkin' you're better
And above all
Only God rises above
Not your call

Remember that medicine
You'd serve in one's face
Here's your spoon
How does it taste

All your cheatin'
And your lies
Hey, how's your wife
Sorry to hear 'bout your divorce
And how she caught you
And served you in court
Lost the house
And your job
Livin' in someone's basement
Lookin' like a slob

It's funny how life takes a turn
And comes back to you
With a burn
Thinkin' you're better
And above all
Only God rises above
Not your call

Remember that medicine
You'd serve in one's face
Here's your spoon
How does it taste

Hey there
Remember me
I wasn't good enough
Back when we were dating
Had your cake
And ate it too
Could do no wrong
Only God knew

I look back now
What was I thinkin'
You were the loser then
And I'm the one winnin'
Puttin' people last in your life
Well, I'm in first place
Remember my face
When I think of yours
I'll bow my head and pray
Here's your spoon
How does it taste

"Fire It Up"

Fire it up
Turn it to high
It's time to grill
Get outside
Fire it up
Ain't nothin' like the smell
Of charcoal and propane
That cookin' done well
Fire it up

Get out the
Table cloth in red plaid
Paper plates gotta have
Condiments
Bring 'em all
Ketchup, mustard, barbecue sauce
Potato salad
Corn on the cob
Steak, shrimp, or chicken kebabs
Hamburgers and hot dogs
Grab a bun
Open a cold one
Under the sun
Fire it up

Turn it to high
It's time to grill
Get outside
Fire it up
Ain't nothin' like the smell
Of charcoal and propane
That cookin' done well
Fire it up

Sweet tea and lemonade
On a lawn chair
Wearin' shades
Sippin' from a Mason jar
Water balloon fight
In the yard
By the pool
Music playin'
Jump right in
Misbehavin'
Watermelon in a triangle
Repel mosquitoes
With a candle
Time to get this barbecue turned up
Grab an apron
Fire it up

Turn it to high
It's time to grill
Get outside
Fire it up

Ain't nothin' like the smell
Of charcoal and propane
That cookin' done well
Fire it up

"Mirror, Mirror"

Mirror, Mirror
As you hang on that wall
With a fairy tale rhyme
Known by all
Crystal clear lookin' back at me
If you could speak
What do you see

Mirror, Mirror
As I put on my makeup
Brush my teeth
And rub on a face scrub
Blow dry and style my hair
Through the shower steam
From which you stare

Mirror, Mirror
What would you say
From all that you see
The things I share between you and me
Would you show the same reflection
And point out every imperfection
Or would you blur out like a filter
And enhance what should be altered

Mirror, Mirror
As you hang on that wall
You never lie
And know it all
If only the world could see your view
And find its comfort lookin' back at you

Mirror, Mirror
Without you we would never know
The truth behind every soul
The beauty behind our reflection
Lookin' back at us with perfection

"American Pastime"

A one, a two, a three
Stand up and sing
In the bleachers
Or in the stands
Grab your friend
With a beer in your hand

Flag wavin' in the wind
The line-up ready in the bullpen
Fans are cheerin'
Grab a mit
Is it a foul, or a hit

There's nothin' like a summer game
Seats are packed from all who came
Young and old in their prime
Sharin' the American pastime

Makin' memories and havin' fun
Prayin' for a homerun
Reminiscin' back in the day
When Babe, Joe, and Mickey would play
Traded cards of all the great ones
And compare who had the most runs

Not just a game
But a piece of history
Whether you're a Yankee or from Wrigley
No matter on which side
Fans cheer for their American pastime

And every time I'm at a game
The memory lives on in his name
A one, a two, a three
The seventh inning stretch with Harry
The "W" flyin' high
Chicago's American pastime

"Daisy"

You're not as popular as the rest
Rose and lily are the usual request
At a ceremony or delivered to someone's door
The others are what they usually look for

Sweet daisy you're my favorite
I even wear you on my bracelet
Your pretty petals
There's nothin' like you
On my heel
I have you tattooed

He loves me, he loves me not
Girls pull your petals
As they thought
You're like a ray of sunshine
With your yellow center
Always make the day
Brighter and better

There's nothin' 'bout you that's cliché
You fill my heart
In a bouquet
You add beauty to any room
Or outside during spring in full bloom

Daisy and all your beauty
You're the prettiest
Absolutely

"Light Beer"

These days
Everyone's thinkin' green
Organic
High protein
Wanna party
Can't hang
Drunk off one
Weight gain
Don't you worry
Have no fear
Grab yourself a light beer

Go 'head
Raise 'em up
Long neck
Solo cup
Light weights
Party's here
Grab yourself a light beer

Got your favorite
On tap
Pale ale
Where it's at
Frosted mug
Gettin' fancy
Outdoors
Summer Shanty
Gettin' tipsy
Vision ain't clear
Grab yourself a light beer

Go 'head
Raise 'em up
Long neck
Solo cup
Light weights
Party's here
Grab yourself a light beer

Saturday night
Party time
Grab a cold one
Put down the wine
Boots out
On the floor
Leave your worries
At the door
Ain't no hangover
Happenin' here
Grab yourself a light beer

Go 'head
Raise 'em up
Long neck
Solo cup
Light weights
Party's here
Grab yourself a light beer

"These Here Boots"

Here's a story about a girl
Who made a life
Into two worlds
One in gym shoes
On the asphalt
And one in boots
Through the cornstalks
Her gym shoes had grown the roots
And planted the seeds
In these here boots

It ain't easy
Walkin' round
In new kicks
On new ground
The soil's fresh
Nothin' grown
Gotta water
This new home
It's time to recruit
The new footprints
In these here boots

Flip flops and peep toes
Ain't practical
On these dirt roads
A train or a cab
Whatever's faster
To pickup trucks
And John Deere tractors

It ain't easy walkin' round
In new kicks
On new ground
The soil's fresh
Nothin' grown
Gotta water
This new home
It's time to recruit
The new footprints
In these here boots

Now even though her shoes retired
Her steps taken have inspired
Roots grow so deep
That helps the stems
Sprout new seeds
Seeds planted in her new shoes
On this new soil
In these here boots

"Blink"

Blink
Open your eyes
What do you see
Is everything the same
Did it all leave

Blink
Open your eyes
How do you feel
Is everything the same
What seems real

Blink
Without a warnin'
The sky is fallin'
Starts stormin'

Blink
Comfort eyes
Starrin' back at you
Say goodbye

Blink
What time is it
Where did it go
What did you miss
You're how old

Blink
Open your eyes
What do you see
Are you surprised

Blink
Open your eyes
Where are you now
What passed you by

Blink
Open your eyes
Do you recognize this life
Do you see God
Stoppin' by

Blink
Close your eyes
Life flew by
Say goodnight

"Own Your Silver"

Second place
Who can relate
Tryin' to reach for number one
Then it all becomes just for fun
Just when you thought
You were ahead
Someone else shows up instead

Gold may be shiny with all its beauty
But can lack in practicality
Not all steaks have to be filet
The taste is in how it's made
You don't have to wear the latest fashion
Even Dolly Parton wore a homemade jacket
It's not about bein' popular
It's about what you deliver
So pop that collar and
Own your silver

Didn't hear them call your name
No certificate or award
Feelin' lame
All that hard work chasin' after
Somethin' you love that really matters
Just when you thought
You were at the top of the charts
Someone else at the table
Flips a higher card

Gold may be shiny with all its beauty
But can lack in practicality
Not all steaks have to be filet
The taste is in how it's made
You don't have to wear the latest fashion
Even Dolly Parton wore a homemade jacket
It's not about bein' popular
It's about what you deliver
So pop that collar and
Own your silver

Let the world see all that talent you harness
And your experience when you tarnish
You don't need recognition to be a winner
Be proud and
Own your silver

"Get It Away"

Out to dinner
Gettin' ready to order
A nice piece of steak
Medium-well
But then I could tell
What's been put on my plate
I swear it was still movin'
Think I even heard it mooin'
Blood red all the way
Just gotta say
Get it away

Now I know y'all might disagree
But some things just ain't feelin' me
Those things that give me a chill
One look turnin' me ill
That makes me gotta say
Get it away

Easter Sunday
Home with the family
At grandma and grandpa's house
Sat down to eat
What do I see
A head of lamb lookin' back at me
Big round eyes
Teeth still inside
A recipe from the old country
Move outta the way
Just gotta say
Get it away

Now I know y'all might disagree
But some things just ain't feelin' me
Those things that give me a chill
One look turnin' me ill
That makes me gotta say
Get it away

Watchin' a movie
Things gettin' spooky
I start to cover my face
A man with a saw
What's comin' outta that wall
And a clown down in a drain
I heard a scream
Realized it was me
Feelin' some major chest pain
Lookin' away
Just gotta say
Get it away

Now I know y'all might disagree
But some things just ain't feelin me
Those things that give me a chill
One look turnin me ill
That makes me gotta say
Get it away

"Ma and Pop Shop"

A clothing boutique
Vintage antiques
A bakery
Or distillery
A rug for your floor
Or wall decor
Like a little treasury
Those little places
We drive by and never stop
Nothin' like a
Ma and Pop shop

On a corner
Or down a main street
Need hardware
Or a place to eat
Fresh spices
Homemade honey
A frosted cupcake
And ground coffee
Ice cream
On a cone or in a cup
Nothin' like a
Ma and Pop shop

Ma and Pop
Win us over
They're the real business owners
They offer everything they have
All made with their bare hands
Offers us somethin'
That can't be replaced
The sweat off their brow
The blood in their veins
Authentic gifts
Of what God gave

Reminds us all
Of the things we forgot
Nothin like a
Ma and Pop shop

"Shootin' the Breeze"

It's one of those days
Sittin' back
Things goin' your way
Breathin' in all that fresh air
Feet up without a care
Rockin' back on a porch swing
Just you and me
Shootin' the breeze

Let's go down by the river
In a boat
And just float
Paddle through
The peaceful water
As we drift
Without a bother
Puttin' my mind at ease
Just you and me
Shootin' the breeze

Can we just stay like this forever
As life stands still
Be still together
Watch the clouds pass us by
The birds flyin' low
From the sky
Stay like this without a try
Days like these
Just you and me
Shootin' the breeze

"You Got a Lemon"

You think you found the one
But it ain't that sweet
A little more sour
Not much of a treat
Thinkin' that yellow glow
Is all sunny and bright
Until you take a bite
From that rind
Your eyes start to water
Sorry darlin'
That ain't no watermelon
Sometimes hell could be mistaken for heaven
It looks like
You got a lemon

Go 'head
Spit out that bad seed
A little more sweet
Is what you need
Not all the ones you pick
Will be right
Next time try to find one
A little more ripe
The outside
May look like heaven
Just to find out
You got a lemon

Don't you cry
We've all been there
And survived
Down the road
You might be surprised
When life gives you lemons
Don't make lemonade
Get rid of it
And make a trade
There's a lot more to pick from
Use your discretion

Don't give up
Just because
You got a lemon

"Wrap-around Porch"

My little apartment
Perfect for my dog and me
With a small balcony
Next to a cherry blossom tree
So sweet and so peaceful
With a farmhouse theme
Lookin' over a courtyard
With lamp post lighting

Sometimes I sit out there
And start to wonder
About my first house
And where it would be
Don't need one now
It's just me

But one day
I'll make that move
And create a home
Maybe for two
And maybe two
Will turn into more
When that time comes
To open that door
Somethin' to look forward to search
A new home hugged by a
Wrap-around porch

Sweet country shutters
Two stories high
A chimney to build a fire inside
Sliding windows
And a picket fence
A big yard
For the dog to play fetch

A fan spinnin' low on the ceilin'
With soft lighting
Givin' all the feelin's
Can't wait to light that torch
A home hugged by a
Wrap-around porch

The American Dream
Everyone thinks about
What that could be
One might look different
Than some of the others
It's the love that's put into it
By our sisters and brothers
No matter how big or how small
Be proud of that arch
Maybe one day
Mine will be hugged by a
Wrap-around porch

"Wednesday"

Our hands are wrinkled
Our hair is white
Hard of hearin'
Losin' our eyesight

Our teeth are false
Our shoes are velcro
Wind breakers
Movin' slow

I wanna sing with you on a Sunday
Askin' God to bless us
At this age
Start off our week
With our routine
Coffee in the mornin'
At night, a hot cup of tea

Saturdays we go walkin' at the mall
Take out our walkers
With the tennis balls
Always look forward
To the middle of the week
Head to our favorite diner
And go out to eat
I'll hold your hand each and every day
And share my discount with you
On a Wednesday

Our pills are in boxes
Socks to the knee
Hard candy in our pockets
Tissue up our sleeve

Wearin' our house shoes
With our house coat and robe
Hair rollers
And Old Spice cologne

Lookin in each other's eyes
Through the line in our lens
A partner in life
'Til the very end

I wanna sing with you on a Sunday
Askin God to bless us
At this age
Start off our week
With our routine
Coffee in the mornin'
At night, a hot cup of tea

Saturdays we go for a walk at the mall
Take out our walkers
With the tennis balls
Always look forward
To the middle of the week
Head to our favorite diner
And go out to eat
I'll hold your hand each and every day
And share my discount with you
On a Wednesday

"Share My Spaghetti"

I once saw in a movie
Made by Disney
Two dogs that fell in love
Sittin' outside
Lookin' into each other's puppy dog eyes
Eatin' pasta under the moonlight

The cartoons know what's up
It could be so easy
Fallin' in love
It's what happens after you fall
That seems to be the hard part
How to make it last
After you open your heart

Just like the movie
Any Italian will tell ya
It's in the cookin'
Since the beginning of time
Love comes from the kitchen
With a glass of wine

Just like food
Love brings us together
Even Jesus ate with friends
At the Last Supper
Two dogs kissin'
To Bella Notte
Where I come from
That's Amore

I'll cook for you my recipe
Sit under the stars and
Share my spaghetti
Love will be there forever
The spaghetti is what holds it all together

"Fall"

The air is crisp
Gloss on my lips
Long sleeves
Fallin' leaves

Halloween
Get dressed up
Pumpkin spice
In my cup
Apple pickin' and hayrides
Apple cider
And Apple pie

Oh how I love this time of year
A time to give thanks
And knowin' Christmas is near
Slip on my boots
And some flannel
Watch football
And light a candle

Scarecrows on the front lawn
A corn maze at the farm
Sit by a bonfire
Makin s'mores
Trick or Treaters at your door
Eatin' all the candy corn

Sit down with the ones you love
For that special meal
Give grace to God
And all the feels
This time of year is always remembered
September, October, and November

"Give It to God"

The world would be a better place
If we all give it to God
And walk away
Give it to God
Everything will be ok
Life is too short to carry hate
Give it to God
And have faith

Back is up against the wall
Wanna fight
And show'em all
Don't wanna decide
Between right and wrong
Don't have the courage to stand tall

You have the power to stand up and say
Turn it around so it goes your way
Tomorrow is always a new day
Give it to God
And walk away

Battlin' illness or an addiction
Givin' up hope
And all love and affection
Fallin' short to the disorder
Consume and take over
Don't have the strength
To move forward

You have the power of your own mindset
Face the challenge that was thrown your way
Tomorrow is always a new day
Give it to God
Everything will be ok

Brothers and sisters makin' you cry
Wanna shut the world out
And hide
Wishin' bad upon the ones who hurt you
With an evil eye
Can't find the peace
Deep inside

You have the power of your emotions
Take a step back
Think of them when you pray
Tomorrow is always a new day
Life is too short to carry hate
Give it to God
And have faith

"That Winter Snow"

Rosy cheeks
Ice hangin' from the trees
It's up to your knees
Car is buried underneath

Thirty below
Polar Vortex in Chicago
It's the Midwest - Don't ya know
That winter snow

It's that time of year
Bust out the UGGS
Hat and gloves
But don't you fear
Folks on the plow
Layin' all the salt down
Look out the window
And watch it blow
That winter snow

Ice skatin' outside
Go on a sleigh ride
See all the lights
How the colors shine so bright

Just wouldn't be right
Without that fluffy white
Fallin' from the sky
Build a snowman
Or throw a ball from your hand
And let it go
The wind always blows towards home
That winter snow

"Stuck Inside"

It's the end of March, year 2020
No St. Patrick's Day
No Easter bunny
It's a crazy time, this time of year
A lot of people livin' in fear
There's a virus spreadin' around the world
People sick and dyin'
From what's been confirmed
Grocery stores are empty
Everythin' bought in sight
Preparin' for what may come
And bein' stuck inside

Businesses closed
Parking lots strayed
People at home wonderin'
How their bills will get paid
Doctors and nurses workin' round the clock
Tryin' to get through the chaos and mental shock
No school or graduation
A shutdown throughout the nation
Tryin' to stay positive
Hopin' things will subside
Takin' care of ourselves
While being stuck inside

Bein' stuck inside is a time to give grace
Come together through the challenges we face
It's not a time for fear to take over
To elevate our strengths
And bring us closer
Deliver the good will that God gave us
And shine the light on our purpose
This life is too precious to just throw away
Unlike toilet paper, we're here to stay
We are too strong to just run and hide
We can face anything
Even stuck inside

"He Must Really Miss You"

Love works in mysterious ways
Sacrifice and faith
Even when it doesn't feel ok
Tryin' to understand
To help see it through
Askin' why do bad things always happen to you

God gave us mothers
But not the kind from birth
With His name imprinted
Reflecting their worth
Cinderella had one
To help pull her through
But that fairytale
Ain't got nothin' on you

Married your high school sweetheart
Never grew apart
More than just an uncle
Always in my heart
You spent most of your life
Helping him through
With your sacrifice and faith
He would have never made it without you

Then God stepped in and gave you both relief
From the constant chemo and radiation
And the tube you had to feed
God closed his eyes in peace
And he fell asleep

Today I heard the news
The cancer got you too
He must really miss you

Can't blame him for tryin'
Up there without his girl
Lookin' down on you
In this crazy world

It doesn't make sense
After all you been through
How could this happen to you too
You see, you were put in his life for a reason
To give him a life that was full
And make you seasoned
This road block is not the same path
It's God's way of showing you
The strength you have

Love works in mysterious ways
Sacrifice and faith
Even when it doesn't feel ok
Tryin' to understand
To help see it through
Askin' why do bad things always happen to you

Godmother is not just a name
It's a virtue
I know in my heart
You are going to pull through

"Bibbidi Bobbidi Boo"

I love you

Printed in the United States
By Bookmasters